This Howie Tale belongs to

Howie Wash Your Paws!

Written by Courtney Chen

Illustrated by Roberto Rivera

Washing your paws is easy you'll see.
It is important to be germ free.

Howie washes his paws throughout the day.
Let's follow him each step of the way!

Wake up, wake up!
You tired pup!
Howie wash your paws!

Paws get wet. Use some soap.
Time to stop? No way, nope.
Scrub, scrub, scrub!
Wash, wash, wash!

Paws all clean! Dry them off!

Well done Howie,
you have clean paws!
Let's give him
a round of applause!

Trottie, trot, trot.
Out for a walk.
Howie wash your paws!

Paws get wet. Use some soap.
Time to stop? No way, nope.
Scrub, scrub, scrub!
Wash, wash, wash!

Paws all clean! Dry them off!

Well done Howie,
you have clean paws!
Let's give him
a round of applause!

Achoo!
Bless you!
Howie wash your paws!

Paws get wet. Use some soap.
Time to stop?
No way, nope.
Scrub, scrub, scrub!
Wash, wash, wash!

Paws all clean! Dry them off!

Well done Howie,
you have clean paws!
Let's give him
a round of applause!

Before you eat
a tasty treat.
Howie wash your paws!

Paws get wet. Use some soap.
Time to stop?
No way, nope.
Scrub, scrub, scrub!
Wash, wash, wash!

Paws all clean! Dry them off!

Well done Howie,
you have clean paws!
Let's give him
a round of applause!

Ewe, sticky!
Gross, icky!
Howie wash your paws!

Paws get wet. Use some soap.
Time to stop? No way, nope!
Scrub, scrub, scrub!
Wash, wash, wash!

Paws all clean! Dry them off!

Well done Howie, you have clean paws! Let's give him a round of applause!

Sprinkle, sprinkle!
Tinkle, tinkle!
Howie wash your paws!

Paws get wet. Use some soap.
Time to stop.
No way, nope
Scrub, scrub, scrub!
Wash, wash, wash!

Paws all clean! Dry them off!

Well done Howie,
you have clean paws!
Let's give him
a round of applause!

Sleepy head!
Time for bed!
Howie wash your paws!

Paws get wet. Use some soap.
Time to stop? No way, nope!
Scrub, scrub, scrub!
Wash, wash, wash!

Paws all clean! Dry them off!

Well done Howie,
you have clean paws!
Let's give him
a round of applause!

You did it Howie! Throughout the day, you washed your paws each step of the way!

Howie is ending the day
with clean paws.
Let's give him a final
round of applause!

Made in United States
North Haven, CT
15 November 2021